WHEN DID YOU ARRIVE?

BY RACHNA SHARMA

WHEN DID YOU ARRIVE?

Copyright © 2021 by Rachna Sharma

No part of this publication may be reproduced, distributed, or transmitted in any form or by any means, including photocopying, recording, or other electronic or mechanical methods, without the prior written permission of the author, except in the case of brief quotations embodied in critical reviews and certain other non-commercial uses permitted by copyright law.

Marigold Publishing Inc.

ISBN
978-1-7775224-2-1 (Hardcover)
978-1-7775224-0-7 (Paperback)

"When did you arrive here?" asked Matthew. Dad looked at Matthew, surprised, and stumped by the question.

"I was born here and have been living here ever since, Matthew. What do you mean?" Dad asked.

Matthew saw that his Dad was confused, after all, he had lived in Canada his whole life. "Well, we are not native to this land. So how did we end up here?" asked Matthew

Matthew's dad finally understood, and continued, "My grandma was only 5 years old when she immigrated to Canada with her parents. She also studied here and got married to my grandpa back then.

I'm a Canadian, my family has been living here for a very long time."

"Oh, now I get it! You arrived here a long time ago when your grandparents arrived in Canada," said Matthew.

Matthew turned to his mother, "When did your family arrive in Canada, Mom?" asked Matthew.

"We came to Canada about 20 years ago. We moved from India."

"My parents wanted me to have a better life than they did. They wanted to live in a place where a comfortable home, education and healthcare would be easily accessible. We moved here to make our lives better," Mom smiled.

"Life for us was difficult in India, and Canada offered us new opportunities. I went to a high school here and learned a lot. I worked in many different places before I found a good job."

As she said this, Matthew could see her getting teary. "I left my friends and family back there and felt very lonely in the beginning. Now I have you and your Dad," she smiled softly.

"Did I tell you that I have a friend at work who has just arrived with her children from Syria because she didn't feel safe there?" asked Mom.

"Why wouldn't she feel safe there?" questioned Matthew.

"There has been a war in their country and people have fled from their homes to find a safer place for their families."

"People leave their home countries and move to different ones for many reasons."

"Some people move to another country temporarily for a few years and then they go back. Some settle into their new country for the rest of their lives," Mom explained.

"I never thought about it until you asked me the question today. You're so right!" Dad chuckled.

"Living in Canada is always exciting because people arrive here all the time, Matthew."

Mom held Matthew's hand, looked at him and smiled, "I know what you mean Matthew.
It doesn't matter when or how long ago... most of us have arrived here in some way, at some time."

Except for the Indigenous peoples in Canada, we each have a history that brought us to this land, which we now share.

Most of us have arrived in Canada in one way or another. When did you arrive?

About the Author

Rachna Sharma has taught for over 25 years in India, Middle East, and Canada. Her many years of work with children has enriched her literary sensitivity. She continues to share her passion for sharing the voices of young children.

As an immigrant, she loves Canada's diversity and would like to add more books with cultural variation on the shelves of kids' libraries at home and school. She currently teaches and lives in Ontario.

A Note to Teachers

Canada is a country of Immigrants. According to Statistics Canada, more than one in five Canadians are foreign-born[1]. Most of the population in Canada has arrived here at some point of time. With such an influx of immigrants, we need literature in schools to address such concepts in a child-friendly way. This story can help spark discussions in classrooms to develop a better understanding of Canadian diversity.

Connections to Classroom Teaching:
In Canada, every family has a story to share. A story of moving to a new country, making a home in new place. It is important for our children to acknowledge and appreciate Canada and its diverse population.

Before Reading:
- Use the cover page and ask students to make predictions, and to question and wonder. What does it mean to arrive? Discuss their perceptions.

During:
- Why does Matthew's mom say, "Life for us was difficult in India". What kind of difficulties do people face in day-to-day living in some countries?
- Why does Matthew's mom get emotional when she talks about leaving her family and friends behind and starting her life in Canada? Do you think she is not happy in Canada?
- Why do people immigrate to a new country?
- Encourage students to research the statistics about immigration in Canada.
- Who lived in Canada before any of the immigrants arrived?

After Reading:
- Students can interview families and ask questions, such as the ones below:
  - When did your family arrive? Was it your parents, grandparents, great grandparents or someone else?
  - Who immigrated to Canada first? When? Why? How?

---
[1] According to data collected from Canada's 2016 Census, 21.9% or 1 in 5 people reported that they were or had been an immigrant or permanent resident in Canada.
Citation:
"Immigration and Ethnocultural Diversity: Key Results from the 2016 Census." Statistics Canada, www150.statcan.gc.ca/n1/daily-quotidien/171025/dq171025b-eng.htm?indid=14428-1&indgeo=0. Accessed 28 Jan. 2021.

www.ingramcontent.com/pod-product-compliance
Lightning Source LLC
Chambersburg PA
CBHW051121110526
44589CB00026B/2999